Playing the Market
the
Stocks and Bonds

DANIEL CONDON

Heinemann Library
Chicago, Illinois

Designed by Herman Adler Design
Photo Research by John Klein
Printed and bound in the United States by Lake Book
Manufacturing, Inc.

07 06 05
10 9 8 7 6 5 4 3 2

Library of Congress Cataloging-in-Publication Data
Condon, Daniel, 1958-
  Playing the market : stocks and bonds / Daniel Condon.
    v. cm. – (Everyday economics)
Includes bibliographical references and index.
Contents: The economy – Savings and investment – Types of
savings – Types of businesses – Stocks – Bonds – Interest rates
– The role of the government – The federal reserve – The
stock market – The stock exchanges – The bond market –
Reading a stock table.
  ISBN 1-58810-495-8 (Library Binding-hardcover) -- ISBN
1-58810-958-5 (Paperback)
 1. Stocks–Juvenile literature. 2. Bonds–Juvenile literature.
3. Saving and investment–Juvenile literature. [1. Stocks.
2. Bonds. 3. Saving and investment.] I. Title. II. Series.
  HG4553 .C66 2003
  332.63'2--dc21

                          2002013698

Acknowledgments
The author and publisher are grateful to the following for
permission to reproduce copyright material:
Cover photograph by ImageBank/Getty Images.
Title page, p. 41B Kathy Willens/AP Wide World Photos; p.
4 Nicole Katano/Brand X/PictureQuest; p. 5 Barry
Winkler/Index Stock Imagery/PictureQuest; p. 6 SW
Productions/Index Stock Imagery/PictureQuest; pp. 7, 28
Rob Crandall/Stock Connection/PictureQuest; pp. 8, 15
Michael Newman/PhotoEdit; p. 10 Image
Source/ElektraVision/PictureQuest; p. 11 Michael
Brosilow/Heinemann Library; pp. 12, 36B Bruno
Joachim/Index Stock Imagery/PictureQuest; p. 13 AP Wide
World Photos; p. 14 Tony Freeman/PhotoEdit; p. 17 Greg
Wahl-Stephens/AP Wide World Photos; p. 18 Image
Bank/Getty Images; p. 19 Stone/Getty Images; p. 22 Susan
Van Etten/PhotoEdit; p. 23 The Granger Collection; pp. 24,
33, 41T Bettman/Corbis; p. 25 Corbis; p. 27 James
Frank/Stock Connection/PictureQuest; p. 29 Charles
Shoffner/Index Stock Imagery/PictureQuest; p. 30 Dave
Pickoff/AP Wide World Photos; p. 32 Ron Frehm/AP Wide
World Photos; p. 34 Comnet LTD/eStock
Photography/PictureQuest; p. 36T Toshiyuki
Aizawa/NewsCom; p. 39 David Young-Wolff/PhotoEdit; p.
43 Peter Beck/Corbis; p. 45 The New York Times.

Every effort has been made to contact copyright holders of
any material reproduced in this book. Any omissions will be
rectified in subsequent printings if notice is given to the
publisher.

Note to the Reader: Some words are shown in
bold, **like this.** You can find out what they mean
by looking in the glossary.

Contents

The Economy

People often refer to "the **economy**." An economy describes the activities of daily life. People work and produce things, and then spend money to buy things. The total of all the things produced by all the people in the United States is called the **Gross National Product (GNP)**. The GNP measures the value of all the **goods** and **services** produced in a given year. It measures the size of the U.S. economy. Factories, stores, restaurants, banks, and workers are all part of the economy.

One way to look at the economy is to divide it into two parts: households and businesses. Households are were people live. People may live in a house, an apartment, or a trailer. Some people may even live on a houseboat. Families

Everyone is part of the economy—even children! Children who receive **allowances** can either save or spend their money. When they spend their money, it enters the economy.

are members of households, as are single people. A business is a place where people work. It may be a factory that produces cars or an office that helps people get insurance. A restaurant, bank, and grocery store are all examples of businesses. People work in businesses and produce goods and services. Goods may include cars, clothes, toys, and food. Services may include medical practices, schools, and housekeepers.

Working for a living

When people produce things for businesses, they earn money. The total amount that they earn is called income. People use income to buy the things they need or want. They pay their rent or **mortgage,** buy food, and go on vacation. The way businesses and households interact can be seen in the circle shown below.

On one side of the circle are households; on the other side are businesses. Households provide workers for businesses. These workers produce goods and services for the economy. They are paid **wages** for their efforts. Businesses produce goods and services for the economy. They sell these goods and services to households. A households uses the money it earns to buy goods and services.

The total value of goods and services is the size of the economy. It can be measured either by the amount paid for goods and services, or by the amount earned by workers.

money from selling goods & services

goods & services market

payment for goods & services

goods & services supplied

goods & services demanded

Businesses

workers produce goods & services

workers supplied

Households

costs to produce goods & services

worker market

wages paid to workers

Savings and Investments

Sometimes, people may not spend all of their **income.** The difference between what people earn and what they spend is called savings. If someone earned $1,000 and spent $900, he or she would save $100. You may receive an **allowance** once a week for doing chores around the house. Some weeks you may spend all of your allowance. Other weeks you may save some of your allowance. You may save for several weeks to buy a game or a toy.

People save for all kinds of reasons. One reason to save is to buy something in the future. A vacation, new furniture, or a new television are all things for which people might save. People also save for emergencies—sometimes things happen that people do not expect.

Families save money for many reasons. One of the most common reasons that families save money is for vacations.

Most businesses today spend money to buy computers for their employees. Businesses usually do this to make work easier.

Someone could become sick or their car could break down. Another reason people might save is because they expect to have a big expense in the future. Many parents save money so that they can pay for their children to go to college. People also save for when they get older, and are not be able to work and produce income. They will **retire** and will need money to live on. Even though they are not working, they will still have to buy food, medicine, and clothing.

When people earn money, they either spend it or save it. If people spend money, it goes to the businesses that make the things they buy. When they save their money in a bank, it goes to another **sector** of the **economy.** In this sector, businesses borrow people's savings from banks to make **investments.**

Businesses spend money on investments to help the business grow. There are many different types of investments. A company may want to build a new factory or warehouse; it may need a new computer system; or it may have to buy some new equipment. A store may want to expand its space. or a company may want to train its workers to perform new jobs. All of these examples require businesses to spend money. This expense is in addition to the usual spending on workers' **salaries** and raw materials.

Delivering pizzas requires that a person or business invest in a car. The hope is that the money made from delivering pizzas will help pay for the car and other business expenses.

If a business is going to stay around or grow, then it must make **investments.** Machinery wears out, buildings grow old, and new and better equipment is invented. Businesses need to have the newest and best equipment in order to compete with other businesses. Imagine a pizza place that delivered pizzas on bicycles instead of in cars or trucks. Even if the delivery person rode very fast, the pizza would still be cold by the time it reached your house. You would not buy pizzas from that place again, and neither would anyone else. The pizza place would go out of business unless it invested in a car or truck for deliveries.

By **investing,** businesses help themselves grow. People in households can also make investments. For them, investing is a way to make their savings grow. People in households might invest their money in businesses, in things like houses or collectibles, or even in the government. People try to invest in things that will increase in value.

Leakages and injections

Think of the economy as a circle. A person's savings can be seen as a **leakage.** This means that by saving money, a person is taking that money out of the economy. Investments, on the other hand, can be seen as injections into the economy. That is, when a person invests in a business or anything else, they are putting new money into the economy.

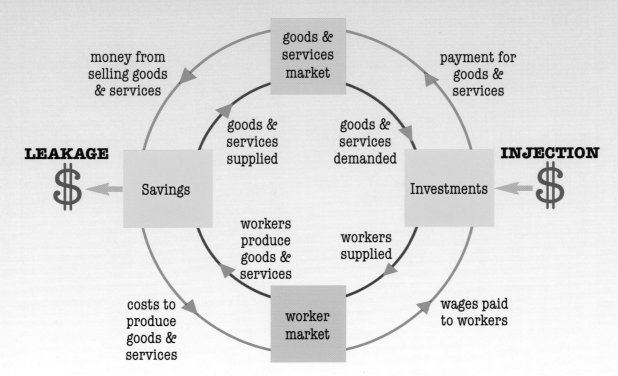

Types of Savings

There are many different things for people to do with their savings. One possibility would be to just pile up the money. Suppose that a person received a $1,000 check for a week's work from the company for which he or she works. He or she goes to a bank and cashes the check into ten $100 bills. He or she then spends $900 that week and takes the other $100 and puts it in a piggy bank. If a person does that every week for a year and does not take any money out, then at the end of the year he or she would have saved $5,200.

There are better ways to save, however. One of the easiest ways to save is a passbook savings account at a bank. A passbook savings account allows people to make **deposits** and **withdrawals** as often as they like. This type of account also earns **interest.** Interest is a payment that is received by the account holder from the bank for lending money. In this case, a person who opens a savings account is lending money to a bank. Interest is paid as a **percentage** of the total amount in the account.

If a bank paid 5 percent interest per year, a person could earn $5 for every $100 in the account each year. If the bank paid interest once a year and you

Putting your money in a savings account is a much better way to save than with your piggy bank at home, which earns no interest. Just like your piggy bank, you can put money in or take money out of a bank whenever your want. But your savings account is safer than a piggy bank. Unlike a piggy bank, a savings account cannot be lost or stolen. The biggest difference is that your savings account grows by itself because of the interest that it earns. The higher the rate of interest that you earn, the faster your money grows.

deposited $1,000 and kept it there, at the end of the year you would have $1,050, including interest. If a bank paid 10 percent interest, then you would earn $10 for every $100 in the account. If you deposited $1,000, you would have $1,100 at the end of the year, including interest.

There are other types of accounts at banks, too. One of the most common is a time deposit, also called a certificate of deposit (CD). This is a type of account where you must leave money in a bank for a certain period of time. CDs are usually offered for periods of 3, 6, 12, 24, or 60 months. CDs and accounts like it earn a higher rate of interest than a regular passbook savings account. These accounts earn higher interest because you cannot withdraw the money until the time period is up. If you have to withdraw the money, you will usually pay a **penalty.**

Another thing that people can do with their savings is to **invest** in **stock.**
A stock is a piece a paper **issued** by a company that represents part
ownership of the company. People purchase stocks from companies or
from other people that own stock. They earn money if the company is
profitable. If a company makes money, it can pay the stockholders a
share of the profit that it earns. This payment is called a dividend.

Stock certificates represent
ownership in a company.
Often, a person will receive
paper copies of stocks like
the ones shown here.

Bonds do not all look the same. Often, the U.S. government will honor an important person in U.S. history by putting a picture of him or her on a bond. This U.S. savings bond is for $1,000 and features Albert Einstein.

Dividends can be in any amount and are paid for each **share** of stock that is owned. Companies do not have to pay dividends. Some companies choose instead to reinvest the money in the company. Companies that do not make profits do not distribute dividends.

People can make money by selling stock for more than they paid for it. However, people can lose money if a company does not do well or if they have to sell the stock for less than they paid for it.

Investing in a **bond** is another thing that people can do with their savings. A bond is a piece a paper issued by a government or by a business that is then purchased by a person. Bonds come in set amounts such as $100, $500, or $1,000. A government or company issuing the bond agrees to pay back the money to whoever bought it at the end of a certain period of time. The length of time can vary anywhere from three months to ten years. A government or company also agrees to pay **interest** until the bond is paid back in full. Usually, the longer time period the bond is for, the higher the interest rate.

Types of Businesses

There are several ways to organize a business. There are three main types of business organizations: **sole proprietorships, partnerships,** and **corporations.**

A sole proprietorship is a business that is owned by a single person. The single owner makes all of the important decisions for a business. Business location, how much a business should grow, and what a business does are a few things a sole proprietor must decide. If a business needs to **invest** more money for new equipment or buildings, the single owner must be able to raise the money alone. He or she might borrow money from friends, a bank, or from his or her own savings. This can be a problem if a owner is unable to borrow the money a business needs. A local restaurant, a flower shop, or a car wash might be examples of sole proprietorships.

Many businesses are owned by families. Sometimes you can spot sole proprietorships because the word *family* is usually a part of the business name.

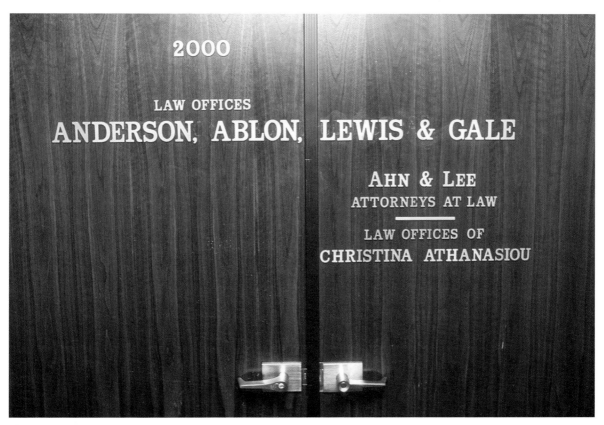

Businesses owned by two people can be easy to spot, too. Look for more than one name in the business name, or for more than one name on the front door of a business.

A partnership is similar to a sole proprietorship except that it has two or more owners. There are many advantages to a partnership. One advantage is that with more than one owner, different skills and talents can be used in the business. Two owners of a pizza place may be able to operate the business more efficiently than one. For example, if there are two owners, one could make the pizzas while the other operates the cash register.

Know It

There are more sole proprietorships than partnerships or corporations in the United States. However, corporations do more business than partnerships and sole proprietorships combined.

Another advantage to having a partner is that it allows an owner to have some time off. A single owner may have to work very long hours. But if there are two people who are equally responsible, they can cover for each other to give each other time off. Or, they can keep the business open for a longer time during the day.

Perhaps the biggest advantage to a **partnership** is the greater ability to raise **investment** money. A single owner, or **sole proprietor,** can only raise as much money as he or she has saved or can borrow. The more partners that are involved, the greater the ability to raise money.

There are many different types of partnerships, but all partnerships have more than one owner. A doctor's office, a realtor, or an accounting firm might be examples of partnerships—though they are just as likely to be sole proprietorships. It depends on how many people are involved in the business and what their relationship is like.

A **corporation** is a very different type of business from a sole proprietor or a partnership. A corporation issues certificates of ownership called **stocks.** People, banks, or companies that buy the stocks are stockholders. They are the owners of the corporation. These stockholders are usually not involved in operating the business. Corporations hire mangers to run the business. If shareholders want to sell their stock they can do so, but the corporation will not be affected.

A big advantage for a business that is a corporation is its ability to raise money. Unlike a sole proprietorship or a partnership, a corporation can raise money by selling stocks. As long as people are willing to buy a corporation's stock, there is no limit to how much money a business can raise. Most big businesses are corporations. Microsoft, Pepsi-Cola, and McDonalds are examples of corporations.

An advantage for stockholders, or owners, of a corporation is that there is less risk for them if a business fails. A person who owns a stock can only lose what he or she invested. If a corporation went out of business and owed a bank one million dollars, the bank could try to collect the money from the corporation. But the bank could not try to collect some of the money from each of the stockholders.

Most large companies are corporations. Nike World Headquarters is located in Oregon. Worldwide, Nike employs more than 22,000 people. Of that, 11,000 employees work in the U.S.

Stocks

There are many different kinds of stocks. Stocks can look different from business to business and from year to year.

Stocks are **shares** of ownership in a corporation. A corporation **issues** stocks in order to raise money for **investment.** Suppose you wanted to start a business making televisions. You would need money for a factory, machinery, computers, and raw materials. You figure out that you will need one million dollars. If you were wealthy, you might have a million dollars in the bank. Perhaps your grandfather is very wealthy and he would give you the million dollars. You could go to a bank for a **loan** of one million dollars. Another way to raise the money would be for you to sell **shares** of stock in your television company.

Know It

Sometimes corporations will announce a stock split. They give shareholders additional shares of stock for each one they own—two for one or three for two. This gives shareholders more stock without having to buy any.

You could issue one million shares of stock and try to sell them for $1 apiece. Or you could issue ten thousand shares and sell them for $100 each. Either way, you could sell shares to raise one million dollars. You would most likely keep some shares of stock in your company so that you would be an owner as well. The people who buy your stock become shareholders, or owners, of your company.

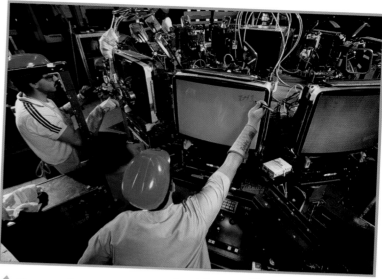

Companies use money raised from selling stock to buy additional equipment. The additional equipment can help make more products for the company to sell.

There are two ways that people can make money when they own stock. One way is if the company whose stock they own makes a **profit.** Suppose the television company you started made a profit of two million dollars in a year and there were one million shares of stock that people had purchased. The profit per share (total profit divided by the number of shares) would be $2 per share. If someone owned 1,000 shares of stock, he or she would make $2,000.

Buying stock

People buy stock as an investment—a way to save money and have it grow. Most people who work and earn **income** can either spend or save their money. There are many reasons for saving. However, the main reason to save is to have money for the future. People want their savings to grow. They want the money they save to make even more money. Investments are a way to earn more money without having to work for it!

Company Profits

+ **Money from investments**
+ **Money from selling goods or services**
− **Costs to produce goods or services**
− **Costs to supply goods or services**
− **Workers wages**
_____

Company Profits

The other way to make money when you buy **stocks** is to sell the stock for more money than you paid for it. Suppose that when you started the television company, someone bought your stock for $1 a **share**. Your television company did very well. People bought more and more of your televisions.

You hired more workers and bought more equipment. Your company grew bigger and bigger. People were now willing to pay $25 for your stock. People who bought your stock for $1 can now sell it for $25. If they owned 100 shares of stock they could sell them for $2,500.

However, there is no guarantee this will happen. The television company may not make any **profits.** If the company does not make any profits, then no profits are given to the shareholders. If the company does not make money, then people will not want to buy its stock. The value of the stock may fall. Instead of the $1 that the person paid for it, the stock may only be worth $0.50. Then the person who bought 100 shares at $1 a share may lose money. They might sell the stock for just $50.

This is very different than putting money in a bank. If you put $25 in a savings account at a bank, it will always be there. There is no danger that the value of your account will be less than $25. However, there is no guarantee that your stock that was worth $25 today will be worth that much next week or even next month. This is why stocks are considered an **investment** that have some risks—there is a chance that a person could lose money.

General Electric Stock Chart

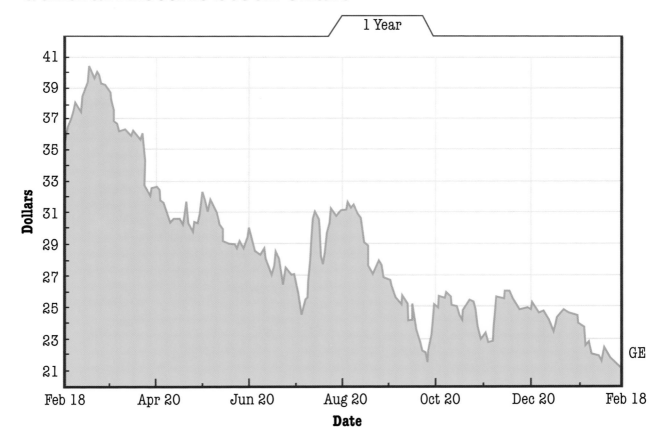

This graph charts the price of one share of General Electric (GE) stock over one year. It is common for the stock of a major **corporation** to decrease and increase in value. Usually, shifts in price have to do with how well the company does and the state of the **economy.**

Bonds

Bonds are similar to stocks. Bonds are a way for a government or business to raise money. A government or business issues a bond for a fixed amount of time and for a fixed rate of interest. They are basically borrowing the money for that time. A $100 bond, for example, might be issued for one year at an interest rate of 5 percent. A person would pay $100 for the bond. One year later, he or she would cash in the bond and receive $100 plus $5 in interest. If it were a five-year bond, he or she would receive the $100 plus $5 per year for each of the five years. The total would be $100 plus $25 (5 years x $5) = $125.

Know It

A bond is different from a stock. A stock is ownership of a company. A bond is a **loan,** with none of the rights or duties of ownership.

Bonds can come in many **denominations**. When a government or a company needs money fast, it issues bonds for people to buy.

BUY WAR BONDS

The U.S. government has often sold bonds to raise money during times of war. The government would make posters meant to encourage people to be patriotic and buy bonds.

There are many different types of bonds. **Corporate** bonds are one type. Companies issue them, usually for a short term of six months or one year. Corporate bond are somewhat risky because there is a chance that the company may go out of business. If this happens, then there is the chance that the people who bought the bonds will not receive their money back. Because this might happen, corporate bonds pay a higher rate of interest than bonds that are certain to be repaid.

Another type of bond is a government bond. Both the **federal** government and local government can issue bonds. Bonds issued by local governments are called municipal bonds. They are less risky than corporate bonds, so they offer lower rates of interest.

Government **bonds** also offer lower rates of **interest** because people do not have to pay **income** taxes on the interest they earn. Most interest is considered income by the **federal** government. People have to pay a **percentage** of the income they earn in taxes to the federal government. The government does not consider interest on local bonds as income. Because people can keep all of the income they earn on these bonds, they are willing to earn less.

The federal government **issues** many different types of bonds. Treasury bonds, treasury notes, treasury bills, and savings bonds are all issued by the federal government. Treasury bonds have a **maturity** of 10, 20, or 30 years. They are issued in $1,000 levels. Treasury notes can be purchased in levels of $1,000 as well, but are issued for periods of one to ten years. Treasury bills are issued for time periods of less than a year. The most common time periods are three or six months. The bond that is most popular in the United States is the savings bond. Savings bonds are issued for as little as $25 for various lengths of time.

The U.S. government encourages people to buy savings bonds. Bonds are a way for the government to borrow money and a way for people to make some money!

Bonds are an easy and safe way to make money—especially government bonds. Only a very extreme and rare situation would cause a government not to be able to pay back its bonds.

Treasury bonds and notes work in a similar way to **corporate** or municipal bonds. You pay whatever the bond or note is worth and then earn the interest. When the time period of the bond is over, you get your money back plus interest.

You can buy savings bonds at a discount. A discount price is a price that is less than the actual value of the bond. For example, you can buy a $1,000 savings bond for $950. One year later, you turn in the bond and receive $1,000. The $50 difference is the interest you earn on the bond.

The risk of **investing** in a bond depends on who issues a bond. The rate of interest is fixed, so there is no risk of changing interest rates. This becomes more important the longer the length of a bond. There is the possibility that a bond will not be paid back. If the company that issued the corporate bond goes out of business, the bondholder may not receive his or her money. There is a slight possibility that a municipality will be unable to pay back its bond. This rarely happens, though. United States government bonds are about as safe as bonds can be. There is almost no chance the government would be unable to pay back its bonds.

Interest Rates

Interest is what you earn when you lend money or what you pay when you borrow money. When you put money in a savings account, you earn interest because you are lending a bank your money. A bank pays you interest because it is borrowing your money. Banks borrow money—through savings accounts—from some people, and lend that money to other people. Banks make money by charging people a higher interest rate to borrow money from the bank than it pays for borrowing money from its depositors.

Suppose you **deposit** $1,000 into your savings account. The bank pays you five percent interest on your money. It lends your money to someone else at seven percent. The bank makes two percent, or $20, in **profit**. It is similar to a grocery store buying bread from a baker for one price and selling it to you for a slightly higher price, making money on the difference.

Choosing between a savings account at a bank and a **stock** or bond is comparable to deciding to whom you would lend your bicycle. Lending your bike to a brother or sister is a safe option—you know you will get the bike back. However, lending your bike to a friend is more risky—there is no guarantee that you will get the bike back.

An important factor in determining interest rates is the risk involved in the **loan.** The higher the risk, the higher the interest rate should be. Another word for risk is uncertainty. When you lend money to a bank by making deposits into your account, you are almost certain to get that money back. If you lent money to a company by purchasing a **corporate bond,** there is a greater chance you may not get the money back. A company would therefore pay you a higher rate of interest. If it paid the same rate as the bank, you would leave your money in the bank, where it is safer. When deciding what **investments** to make, people need to weigh the risks against how much interest they might get.

Another thing that determines interest rates is how long you are lending your money. With a savings account, you can get your money back any time you want. If you bought a one-year bond, however, you would not be able to use your money for one year. You would likely earn a higher rate of interest if you were to buy the bond. If you did not think you would need the money for a whole year, you would probably earn more interest if you **invested** in a bond. If the interest were the same, you could leave your money in the bank, where you could get it any time.

Key Rates			
Percent	**Yesterday**	Day Ago	Year Ago
Federal funds	**1.25**	1.35	1.76
3-month T-bills	**1.16**	1.16	1.71
6-month T-bills	**1.17**	1.17	1.82
10-yr. T-infl.	**1.94**	2.96	3.26
10-yr. T-note	**3.89**	3.95	4.87
30-yr. T-bond	**4.82**	4.87	5.38
Telephone bd.	**5.97**	6.03	7.45
Municipal bds.	**5.06**	5.08	5.27

Many newspapers will publish the interest rates for various types of bonds everyday. A newspaper will usually list interest rates from different days and years so that a person can see how rates have changed.

Know It

The rule of 72

If you want to see how long it would take for your savings to double, divide 72 by the rate of interest you earn. If you earn six percent interest, your savings would double in twelve years (72/6=12). If you could earn twelve percent interest, your money would double in just six years!

The Role of the Government

The government plays a very important role in the **economy.** The government tries to make sure that the economy runs smoothly. One of the ways the government does this is to make laws. The government creates laws so that businesses operate in a fair manner and treat customers the right way. Other laws guarantee that companies do not meet with each other and set high prices. The government also creates laws to ensure that companies produce products that are safe.

When companies **issue stocks,** the government makes sure they follow the laws. In addition, it sees that everyone has the same information about stocks and the companies that issue them. If some people had more information about particular stocks than others, they would have a better chance to make money than the people who did not have the same information.

Tax money is used by the government in many ways. Some money is used to build and maintain government buildings, such as the White House and Capitol.

Local governments are responsible for providing and maintaining schools in its area. Local governments are able to provide education through the tax money they collect from local residents.

The other role of the government is to spend money to keep the economy strong. The government collects taxes from everyone who earns **income.** It gives some of that money to people who do not have any income. It spends money on things that make everyone's life better, such as roads, schools, and hospitals. The government also spends money to help protect the country.

Sometimes the government has to spend more money than it has. If this happens, then it borrows money. The government borrows money by issuing **bonds** to sell to the public. The more money the government has to borrow, the more bonds it sells to people. The way the government encourages people to buy bonds is to raise the **interest** rate on bonds. Higher interest rates make bonds a more attractive **investment** to people.

Know It

The government is a huge part of the economy. More than one-third of all the spending in the United States is done by **federal,** state, and local governments.

The Federal Reserve

The Federal Reserve plays a very important role in the **economy**. The Federal Reserve is the central bank of the United States. Every country in the world, except for a few very small ones, has a central bank. The Federal Reserve System in the United States was formed in 1913. There were central banks before 1913, going all the way back to the founding of our country.

The central bank of a country has many roles. It acts as the government's bank. It makes up and enforces the rules for other banks in the country. The most important role for the central bank is to control the money supply.

The Federal Reserve is the government agency that controls the amount of money

The Federal Reserve System has twelve districts located in different regions of the United States.

in the economy. If you look at a dollar bill, or any paper money, you will notice that written across the top are the words "Federal Reserve Note." The money supply, however, is much more than the amount of **currency** in the economy. A larger part of the money supply is the amount of **deposits** in different accounts in banks. The Federal Reserve has a big impact on how much money is in the banking system. It uses various methods to control the money supply.

The first thing the Federal Reserve does is to determine how much money banks can lend. The Federal Reserve makes this decision based on the size of a bank and how many deposits it has. A bank has to have enough money to give to people who want to make **withdrawals.** Then it can lend out the rest. The greater the amount that banks can lend out, the more money there is in the economy.

Know It

Currency is only a very small part of the money supply. In fact, checking accounts are a much larger part of the money supply.

Federal Reserve symbols

The government uses letters and numbers to identify each of the twelve main Federal Reserve Banks. When paper money is printed, the letter and number of the place where it was printed appears on the bill. These are the letters and numbers used to indicate the Federal Reserve Banks:

Boston, MA	A	1	Chicago, IL	G	7
New York, NY	B	2	St. Louis, MO	H	8
Philadelphia, PA	C	3	Minneapolis, MN	I	9
Cleveland, OH	D	4	Kansas City, KS	J	10
Richmond, VA	E	5	Dallas, TX	K	11
Atlanta, GA	F	6	San Francisco, CA	L	12

The second thing the Federal Reserve does is to buy and sell government **bonds.** If it buys more than it sells, it increases the money supply. This happens because when the Federal Reserve buys bonds, it gives money to those who own the bonds. The people that owned the bonds now have money instead. They can use that money to buy things. They can also put that money in their bank account. The bank can then lend that money to other people who want to buy things.

When the Federal Reserve sells bonds, it receives money from the people who buy the bonds. This means that people have less money to spend. If people take money out of their bank accounts, it means that banks have less money to lend people to buy things. If the Federal Reserve sells more bonds than it buys, it causes the supply of money in people's hands to decrease.

Alan Greenspan has been chairperson of the Federal Reserve System since 1987. The Federal Reserve System earns money from its **investments** and from the fees it charges banks for its services.

About 60 foreign banks and international organizations store gold at the Federal Reserve Bank of New York. The United States, however, stores its gold at Fort Knox in Kentucky (above).

The final tool the Federal Reserve uses to control the money supply is through **interest** rates. By deciding what interest rates should be, the Federal Reserve has a big impact on economic activity. If interest rates are low, more money will be borrowed and eventually spent. People will borrow money to buy houses and cars. Businesses will borrow money to build new factories and buy new equipment. Both businesses and individuals borrow more when interest rates are low because it costs less to borrow. If interest rates are high, people will save more money and spend less. Businesses and households would be less likely to borrow money. At higher rates of interest, the price of borrowing is more.

The Stock Market

The **stock market** is the overall buying and selling of stocks. In any market, there are buyers and sellers. For example, there is a market for cars. There are many different car dealerships that sell cars, and there are many different people who buy cars. All together they make up the market for cars. The same is true for groceries, houses, fast food, and movies. Any situation where there are both buyers and sellers can be considered a market. Markets allow those who want to sell things to sell and those who want to buy things to buy.

The car market could not exist without people to sell the cars and people to buy the cars.

Ice cream and the stock market

When supply is low, sellers have to raise the price of ice cream cones. As the supply of ice cream cones increase, the price decreases. People are likely to buy more ice cream as the price decreases. When supply and demand meet, then everyone is happy with the price.

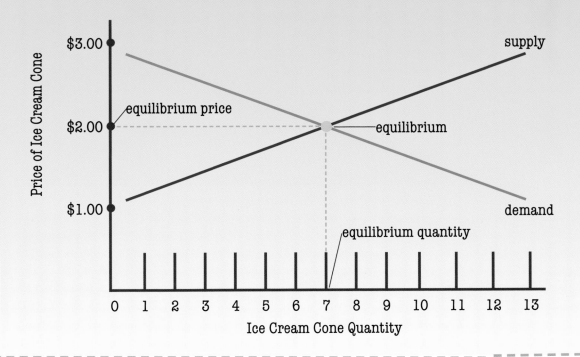

Any market is an exchange of **goods** and **services.** Markets do this by allowing prices to adjust to allow sellers to sell and buyers to buy. Markets are said to tend toward **equilibrium.** This is a situation in which everyone is satisfied. The market heads toward equilibrium by letting prices adjust. If there are more buyers than sellers, there is a shortage in the market. When there is a shortage of something, the sellers will increase the price higher and higher.

Know It

Markets are very efficient. Without any rules or regulations, markets allow people to buy just about any thing they want at the best possible prices.

When a new video game system comes out, there is great demand. People are willing to pay high prices in order to get it. After a while, though, when the excitement wears off, the price lowers so that even more people will buy the system.

A shortage will cause an increase in the number of sellers and a decrease in people who buy. This will continue until the number of buyers and sellers is the same. This is called market **equilibrium.** The opposite happens if there are more sellers than there are buyers. This is called a surplus. Prices will fall and the market will go back to equilibrium. This is how the **stock market** works, too.

Think of a new toy. When the toy first comes out, everybody wants to buy it and the price is very high. After a while, more and more people have bought the toy and fewer and fewer people want to buy it. The price of the toy will fall. The stock market works in a similar way.

There are actually two different types of stock market. One is called the primary market and the other is called the secondary market. The primary market is where **corporations** sell stock. Corporations sell **issues** of **stock** to raise money for their businesses. This is the easiest way for corporations to obtain money for new factories or equipment. As long as people believe that a company will continue to be **profitable,** they will be willing to buy a company's stock.

This is very important for the **economy** because it allows companies to **invest** and grow. As companies grow, it creates more jobs for people. Companies do this in two ways. One way is by hiring more people to work for the company. More people are needed in order to produce more.

The second way is that when companies buy things from other companies, those companies also hire more people to make those things. All these people with new jobs have money to spend. They buy food, cars, and houses. The companies who make food and cars and houses need to hire more people. This makes the economy grow and makes everyone better off.

Know It

The stock market has experienced many declines over the years. One of the biggest was from 1929–1933, also known as the Great Depression. The value of the Dow Jones Industrial Average declined more than 89%! This means that if you had $1,000 in the stock market in 1929, by 1933 the value of your **investment** would be around $110.

The secondary market is where **stocks** are bought and sold among individuals who own stocks. Someone who owns a particular stock sells it to someone else who wants to buy that particular stock. The company that issued the stock has nothing to do with this market. The secondary market is very important for companies, however. Very few people would buy stocks in the primary market if there was not a secondary market where they could sell them. It is also very important for the **economy.** The **stock market** is where many people put their savings. If the value of the stocks in the market grows, people become more wealthy. When they become more wealthy, they will usually spend more money. This causes the economy to grow, providing jobs and **income** for more people.

Dow Jones Industrial Average

It's in the cards

One way to think about the stock market is to think about baseball or Pokemon cards. The store where you buy these cards could be considered the primary market. The secondary market is when you and your friends trade these cards among yourselves.

However, the value of stocks does not always increase. Sometimes the prices of stocks in the stock market fall. This is not good for the economy. People will lose money and therefore will spend less. It also can cause the value of some people's savings to decrease. If someone had invested in the stock market to provide them with money for their **retirement**, they would now have less money with which to retire. This could make them save even more then they were saving before. In order to save more, they would have to spend less. They would buy fewer cars and houses. This situation could cause people to lose their jobs and their income.

The Stock Exchange

The place where most **stocks** are bought and sold is called a **stock exchange.** There are more than 100 different stock exchanges in many different cities around the world. One of the most famous stock exchanges is the New York Stock Exchange (NYSE). It is located in New York City. The American Stock Exchange is also located in New York. The NASDAQ is another stock exchange. It is not in one place, but is traded over computer lines.

Stocks are bought and sold at stock exchanges by **brokers** who represent buyers and sellers. The sellers have a price for which they would like to sell. The buyers, on the other hand, have a price for which they would like to buy. If the two agree, the stock is sold. If they do not, there is no sale. This is an ongoing process. People tell brokers what stock they want to buy and sell. The brokers at the stock exchange then try to do what the buyers and sellers want. If more people want to buy a stock than want to sell it, then the price of the stock will go up. If more people want to sell the stock than buy it, the price will go down.

There are several things that would make people want to sell or buy stocks. A toy company might introduce a new video game that everyone wants to buy. People would want to buy stock of that toy company because they think the company will do well. On the other hand, things can happen that will make people want to sell stock. What if the price of gasoline went up to $10 a gallon? People would probably buy fewer cars. People would then want to sell the stock they had in car companies.

There are also events that have different effects on different companies. What if there was a very rainy, cold summer? Companies that make sunscreen or bathing suits would not do very well. But a company that makes umbrellas would have a very good summer. People might sell their stock in the bathing suit company and buy stock in the umbrella company. It is important to remember that the prices of different stocks move in different directions.

The New York Stock Exchange is always a busy place. Brokers move around a lot as they try to make buyers and sellers happy.

There are ways to look at the **stock market** to get an overall idea of it. One measure is the Dow Jones Industrial Average. It measures on a daily basis the stock prices of 30 of the biggest companies in the United States. This average is reported on the news and in the newspaper. People use this information to see how the **economy** is doing. By keeping track of the Dow Jones over a period of time, people can see whether or not the economy is going to grow in the future.

The Bond Market

The **bond** market is like the **stock market** or other markets—there are buyers and sellers. If more people want to buy than want to sell, prices go up. If more people want to sell than buy, prices go down. If the bond is for a fixed amount, **interest** rates move up or down depending on demand. The bond market, like all markets, will tend toward **equilibrium.**

There are actually different markets for bonds. There is a market for **corporate** bonds and there is a market for government bonds. This is because there are different sellers in the different markets. The bonds have different levels of risk as well.

There is a relationship between bond prices and interest rates. The higher the interest rate, the lower the price of the bond. The easiest way to think of this is to think about bonds that are sold at a discount.

Savings Banks	Money Mkt.	3-mo. C.D.	6-mo. C.D.
Apple Bank	0.40	0.80	0.75
Astoria Fed Savings	0.40	0.75	1.00
Emigrant Savings	1.05	1.01	1.10
GreenPoint Bank	1.25	N.O.	1.25
Hudson City SB (N.J.)	1.50	1.90	2.00
Independence Comm Bank	0.60	1.01	1.11
Investors Savings Bank	1.75	1.90	2.00
People's Bank (Conn.)	N.O.	1.00	1.00
Provident Bank	0.75	1.45	1.60
Queens County Savings Bank	0.75	1.35	1.65
Roslyn Savings Bank	0.35	1.20	1.50
SI Bank & Trust	1.10	1.26	1.31

Interest rates are usually published Monday through Friday in many newspapers. You can find interest rates for stocks, bonds, CDs, and other investments.

Government bonds can come in many **denominations.** It all depends on how much a person wants to spend.

For example, savings bonds and treasury bills are sold at a discount. The discounted price represents the interest you earn. The higher the rate of interest, the lower the bond will cost. If you have a $100 bond that pays 5% interest, and you buy it at a discount, you would pay $95. If it paid 10% interest, you would be able to buy it for $90. When it was time to turn the bond in, you would get the full $100—even if you only paid $90 for it. This is one way that people can make money with bonds.

If more people want to sell bonds then want to buy them, prices go down. This means interest rates go up. If the government wants to sell lots of bonds, for example, interest rates will go up. If the government does not have many bonds to sell, then prices will go up and interest rates will go down. Remember that the government **issues** bonds when it has to spend more money than it has. When the government does this, interest rates increase.

Know It

There really is no limit to how much money the government can borrow. As long as people are willing to buy government bonds, the government can continue to borrow more and more money.

Reading a Stock Table

You can learn how to follow the **stock market** by looking in most newspapers. Start by picking a company with which you are familiar. Find out the symbol for the **stock.** In most newspapers, you will be able to find a stock table Tuesday through Saturday. You can create a table and keep track of how your stock does every week. Maybe some of your friends or classmates will follow the market with you. You can see whose stock does better. If you want to do this by yourself, just pick two or three stocks and see how they do against each other. Find your stock and then obtain the following information:

52 Week High/Low

This column shows both the high and low price for a stock over the last year. You can then tell how the stock is doing today compared to how it did over the past year. Stock prices are sometimes listed in fractions: halves, quarters, eighths, or sixteenths. Fractions represent parts of a dollar. A stock price of 75 1/4 is equal to $75.25.

Stock

The stock column shows an abbreviation of the name of a stock. It is called a stock symbol. It is usually a combination of letters contained in the company name. Every stock has a different symbol. Symbols are listed alphabetically.

Div

This column represents the dividend that a stock pays. A dividend is the payment you can expect to receive for owning the stock for one year. If the number in the column is 3, this means that for each **share** of stock that you own you would receive three dollars. Some companies might not pay dividends. In this case, the column would be blank.

P/E

The P/E column tells you the **ratio** of a stock price to its earnings. It is determined by dividing the price of a share of stock by its earnings per share. Earnings per share is the total **profits** of the company divided by the number of shares of stock.

For example, suppose a company earned a profit of ten million dollars last year. There are one million shares of stock in this company. The earnings per share would be ten million/one million = $10. If the stock in this company is selling for $50, than the P/E ratio would be 50/10=5.

The P/E ratio is an indication of how valuable people think a stock is. A high P/E ratio means that people who are buying the stock believe that the stock is a good **investment** and will make even more money in the future. This ratio is especially helpful if you want to compare companies in a particular industry. A company with the highest P/E ratio in a particular industry may be the company you want to buy stock in.

High, Low, Last

These three columns show the prices of a stock for a given day. The high tells the highest price for the day, and the low the lowest price. The last, or close, is the price of the stock at the end of the day when the market closed. Unless something important happened that day, there will not be much difference between these numbers.

Chg

This column tells you the change in the price of the stock from yesterday to today. If the price went up, there will be a plus sign followed by the dollar amount of the increase. A minus sign means that the price went down by the amount following the minus sign.

Last	Chg	52-Week High	Low	Stock	Div	Yld %	P/E	Sales 100s	High	Low	Last	Chg
72.50	−0.50	28.13	16.05	Pechny	.44e	2.0	...	121	22.75	22.48	22.55	−0.79
52.65	−3.02	48.60	20.70	Pediatrx	...	...	17	4842	28.77	27.50	27.96	−0.57
24.18	+0.01	10.90	9.50	Pengrth gn	2.11e	...	...	199	10.15	10.00	10.13	−0.07
21.30	+0.30	11.53	5.90	PennAm s	.16f	1.5	20	45	10.50	10.45	10.45	−0.06
35.60	−1.36	19.20	14.31	PnnEMA	.32	2.1	cc	13	15.45	15.35	15.35	−0.05
32.37	−0.91	20.75	14.00	PennEM	.32	2.0	cc	144	15.82	15.70	15.72	−0.08
13.97	+0.22	6.85	2.10	PennTrty	...	...	dd	316	4.22	4.05	4.22	+0.06
15.00	−0.20	42.00	26.03	PennVa	.90	2.4	13	601	38.59	38.20	38.22	...
11.96	−0.04	26.25	19.50	PenVaRs n	.84e	4.2	...	145	20.20	20.01	20.10	−0.03
20.79	−0.53	29.50	18.64▼	Penney	.50	2.7	44	39027	18.91	18.04	18.60	−0.54
22.10	−0.42	27.20	18.25	PenRE	2.04	8.3	20	1123	24.88	23.80	24.68	−0.02
46.07	−0.58	21.75	9.00	PenzlQS	.10	0.5	dd	9338	21.65	21.62	21.62	−0.03
44.78	−0.12	49.84	28.40	Pentair	.76f	1.8	63	2267	44.10	41.70	43.10	−0.79
0.95	−0.04	17.80	1.35▼	Penton	...	...	dd	25159	1.28	0.93	1.00	−0.36
1.44	+0.11	42.94	34.35▼	PeopEn	2.08	5.9	15	2787	35.31	34.26	35.10	+0.52
24.85	−0.55	19.39	8.75	PepBoy	.27	2.0	18	x10505	14.25	13.19	13.79	−0.43
38.49	−0.31	34.80	19.83	PepsiBot s	.04	0.1	22	21543	28.37	27.10	27.10	−1.03
17.40	+0.30	10.68	4.05	PepsiGem	.31e	...	...	880	10.20	10.04	10.10	+0.06
35.01	−0.01	53.50	43.60▼	PepsiCo	.60f	1.4	29	144422	44.00	41.21	43.40	−1.21
113.92	−3.19	15.99	11.65	PepsiAmer	.04	0.3	70	2482	13.95	13.18	13.25	−0.73
122.10	−3.00	36.30	9.26▼	PerkElm	.28	3.0	dd	13353	9.50	8.90	9.21	−0.14
21.70	+0.10	14.30	7.85	Perdigao	.80e	8.6	...	52	9.34	9.10	9.34	+0.24
27.45	−0.18	13.79	3.56	PerezCo	...	...	...	4603	6.38	5.75	5.75	−0.59
13.24	−0.16	6.53	4.97	Prmian	.71e	14.0	7	369	5.15	5.03	5.07	+0.04
21.90	+0.29	21.11	9.50	PerotSys	...	...	53	9323	10.58	9.99	10.58	+0.35
41.06	+0.69	1.64	0.40	PersGp	...	...	dd	73	0.85	0.85	0.85	...
25.83	+0.02	28.80	21.16	PetroC g	.20	...	...	118	27.40	26.78	26.89	−0.61
29.80	−0.10	22.48	16.60	PetChina	1.45e	6.8	...	438	21.60	21.18	21.23	−0.22
40.66	+0.72	27.42	15.65	Petrobrs	1.32e	7.6	...	15357	17.46	17.03	17.35	−0.07
11.25	−0.22	26.00	14.00	PetrbrsA	1.66e	10.5	...	8372	15.95	15.48	15.86	+0.04
62.30	−0.18	27.25	21.65▼	PetRes	1.50e	2.0	q	524	21.70	20.75	21.10	−0.70
14.70	−0.55	11.40	2.85	PetrolGeo	...	...	dd	6940	3.41	3.16	3.34	−0.01
17.40	+0.13	37.53	22.50	PfeifVac	.53e	1.8	...	16	29.13	29.12	29.13	−1.98
14.79	+0.07	44.04	30.63▼	Pfizer	.52	1.6	25	315754	32.70	29.75	32.60	+1.57
15.60	+0.01	42.20	15.60	PhmRes	...	...	10	3843	23.24	21.51	23.19	+0.54
15.10	+0.08	47.85	31.08▼	Pharmacia	.54	1.7	18	83114	32.60	30.36	32.17	+0.85
10.06	+0.01	42.51	25.74	PhelpD	...	...	dd	8530	39.30	38.21	39.21	+0.16
14.97	+0.11	25.75	23.80	PhilRet28	1.64	6.5	...	130	25.45	25.24	25.30	+0.05
16.11	+0.03	25.00	18.02▼	PhilaSub s	.53	2.9	21	2606	18.60	17.35	18.01	−0.11
15.22	−0.05	57.79	40.35	PhilMor	2.32	5.3	11	101898	45.15	43.50	44.00	−1.17
16.07	+0.15	14.15	6.07	PhilLD		...	...	611	6.30	6.20	6.22	−0.31
16.55	−0.04	33.00	15.03	PhilipsEl	.31e	1.2	...	7999	25.65	24.17	25.45	+0.34
15.06	+0.11	2.69	1.77	PhillptB	1.25c		7	202	2.10	2.05	2.08	−0.02

Most major newspapers publish stock market tables from the previous day. This section is from *The New York Times*.

Glossary

allowance amount of money given regularly, usually to a child, sometimes in exchange for doing chores

bond loan to a government or business that earns interest

broker person who sells and buys stocks or bonds

corporation company that issues stocks

currency means of exchange; money

denomination one of a series of different values, as with money

deposit to put in, as money into a bank account, or the amount put in

economy use or management of money

equilibrium condition in which opposite forces are in balance

federal describing a union of states that share a government

good thing that can be bought or sold

Gross National Product (GNP) value of all the goods and services produced

income money earned through work or from other sources

interest amount charged for the right to use or borrow money

invest to contribute money to something in order to make a profit

investment act of putting money into a stock, bond, or account in order to earn interest or profit

issue to give out or distribute; when a company sells new shares of stock

leakage when people do not spend all of their income

loan money given to a person with the understanding that it will be paid back with interest

maturity fully grown or developed; in banking, when a bond matures, it is time to turn it in

mortgage money given to a person to buy a house or other piece of real estate with the understanding that it will be paid back with interest

partnership when two or more people own a business

penalty punishment for breaking a rule; in banking, usually involves paying a fee

percentage certain part or number of every hundred

profit money made in a business venture. When a company makes a profit, it is called *profitable*.

ratio relationship between numbers

retire to give up a job, business, or career

salary set amount of money paid for work over a certain period of time

sector part of the economy

service work done for another or others

share one of the equal parts, or stocks, into which ownership of a company is divided

sole proprietorship business that is owned by a single person

stock part ownership of a company

stock exchange particular location where stocks are bought and sold

stock market description of the buying and selling of stocks

wage payment for work based on the number of hours worked or the rate of production

withdrawal to remove, such as money from a bank account

More Books to Read

Burkett, Larry (ed.). *Money Matters for Kids.* Chicago: Moody Press, 2001.

Giesecke, Ernestine. *Everyday Banking: Consumer Banking.* Chicago: Heinemann Library, 2003.

Macht, Norman. *Money and Banking.* Broomall, Penn.: Chelsea House, 2001.

Index